FIRST BOOK – VOL. 1
By
Orlando Hernandez
Political Cartoonist

DESCRIPTION

In America where times and ideas are so rapidly and radically changing, things could get a little challenging. Here is a spin on politically correct from a politically incorrect point of view. This book was compiled by an artist who tries to capture the moment of the current administration.

This volume contains forty-one original, political cartoons presented with artistic skill that has a spin of its own.

DISCLAIMER: This book contains strong language and subject matter, that may be offensive to some readers.

TABLE OF CONTENTS

Description   2

Disclaimer   2

Beginning   3

CHANGE YOU CAN BELIEVE IN!!!!!

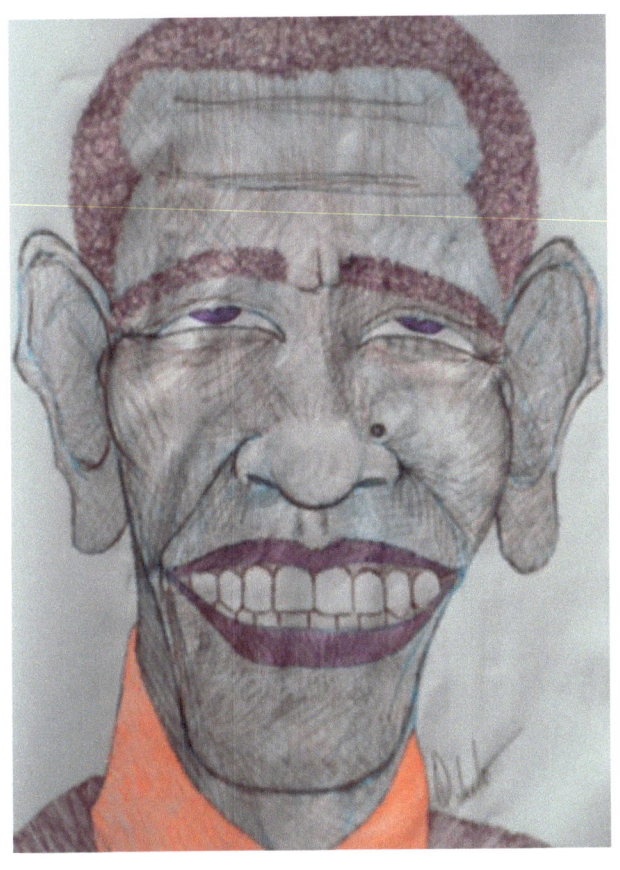

IT'S TRUE!! ... I had sex with CHER'S daughter ... I mean, CHER'S son ... I mean, CHER'S daughter ... I mean ... I don't know what I mean ... BUT!! ... I promise, NEVER TO DO IT AGAIN!!!!!!

I'm bonena put my 14 ½ size fut up yo azz!!!!!

YES, BUT!!... I only wear this on
special HOLY DAYS!!!!

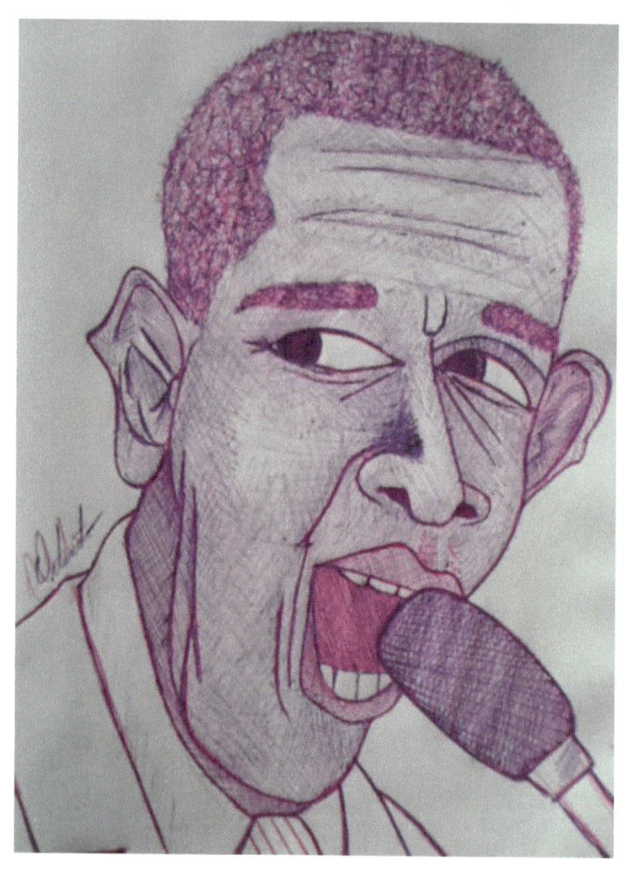

WHY ARE YOU STARING??...
Have you not ever seen a purple Black man!!!

OBAMA/OSAMA …
WHAT'S THE DIFFERENCE????

HMMMMMMM! ... WHAT
CAN I SCREW UP TODAY??

HELLO!! ... GAY HOTLINE???

I always tell the truth … even when I lie!!

I WANT MY CRACK PIPE!!!!!!

I don't have a problem with white people.
I think everybody should own one.

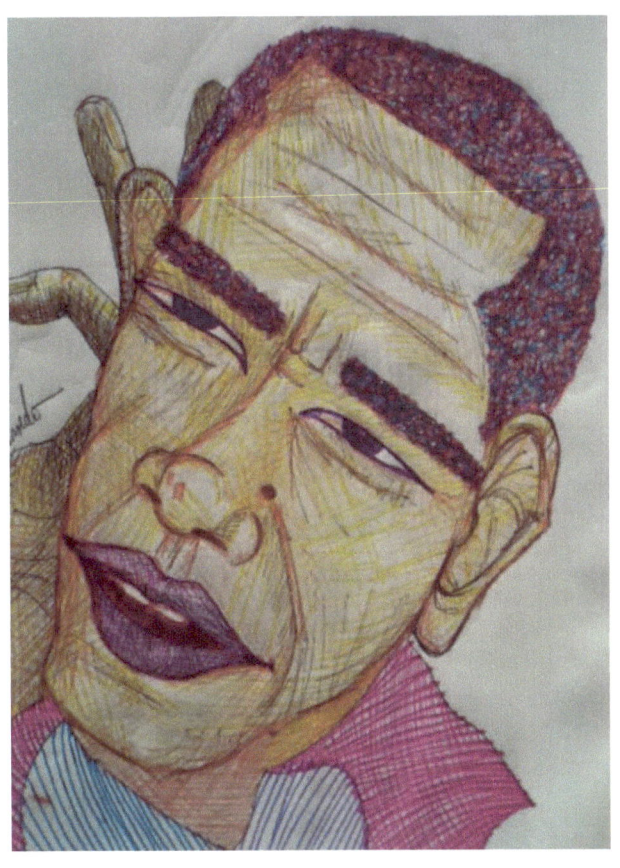

What's that you say?? You're living on food
stamps because there's no work out there!!!!

DEAR GOD! … I want to become a CHRISTIAN!! …
But I don't know how. PLEASE HELP ME!! DEAR JESUS!!!!!

BARACK has been a blessing to the homosexual community. We LOVE OBAMA!!!! He is a god!

ORLANDO!!!!! … Is really getting on my nerves!!

If AMERICANS have no bread ...
they should EAT CAKE!!!!

I'M SO SICK OF THIS JOB!!!!

I'm not only your president … I'm also a CRYPT!!!

Did I say OBAMA-CARE?? ...
I mean ... OSAMA'S HAIR!!

IT'S TRUE!!! ... I had sex with GEORGE W. BUSH
… and his father!!!!!

NOW WHY WOULD ANYBODY
THINK I'M A SOCIALIST????

EVERYBODY WANG CHUNG TONIGHT!!!!!

HELL NO!!!! ... My children WILL NOT
work for minimum wage!!!

DON'T ASK / DON'T TELL!!!!!

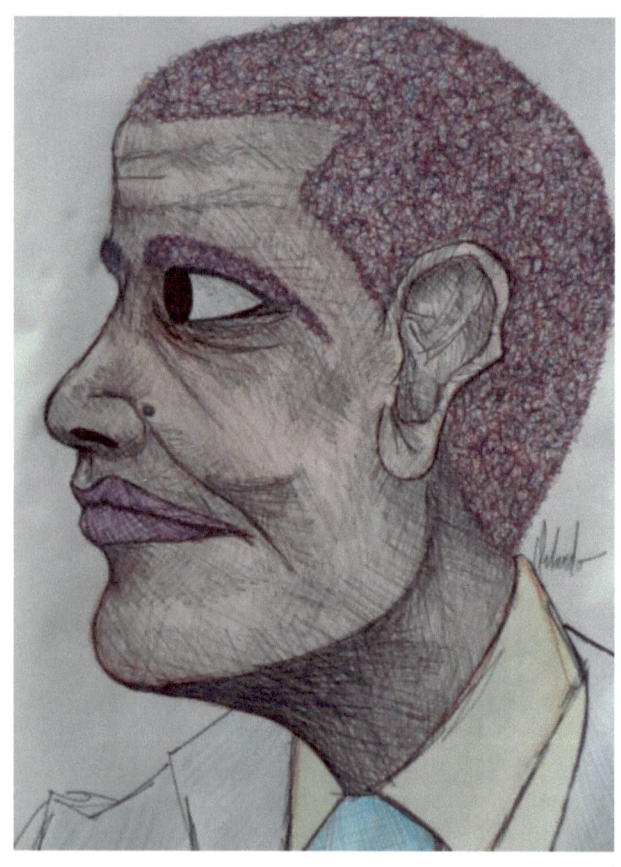

I'm the best black president America ever had!!!!!

I categorically deny having any knowledge of secret
stem cell research taking place in AREA FIFTY-ONE!!!!!!!

IF CONGRESS WOULD ONLY TAKE SOME OF THIS
AND MIX IT WITH SOME OF THAT, WE COULD
HAVE; WHAT I CALL, "KABALECTPOISHTU!!!"
This message was brought to you by THE WHITE HOUSE!!!!

WHAT HAS HE DONE FOR BLACK PEOPLE???
… WHAT HAS HE DONE FOR ANYBODY????

HELLO CHINA! … YOU GOT MY MONEY!!!!!

IT IS WRITTEN!! ... I BE YO NU MASSIAH!!!!!

OBAMA SPEAKS WITH FORK & SPOON!!!!
He has angered the GREAT SPIRIT of AMERICA!!!!

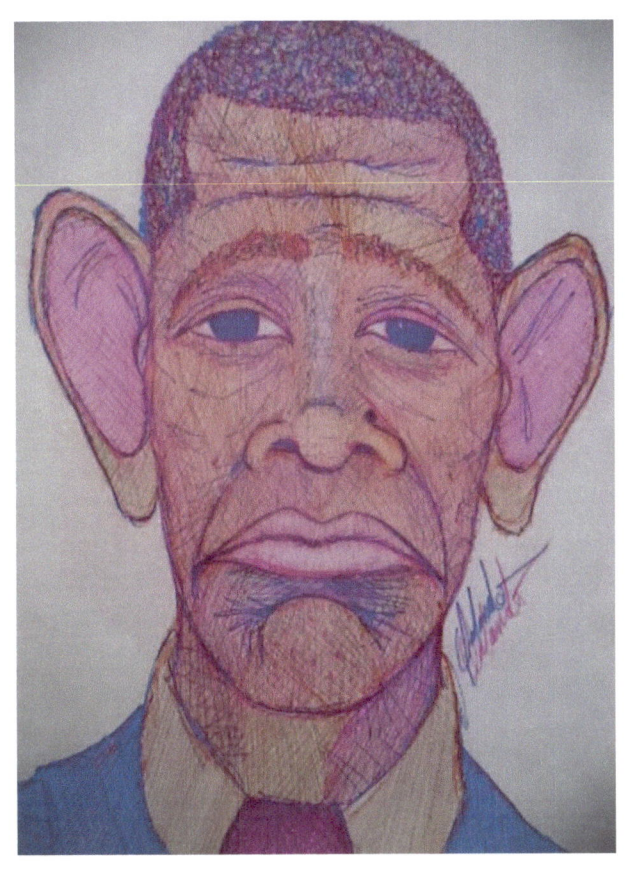

SPEAK UP!!!! ... I'm all ears.

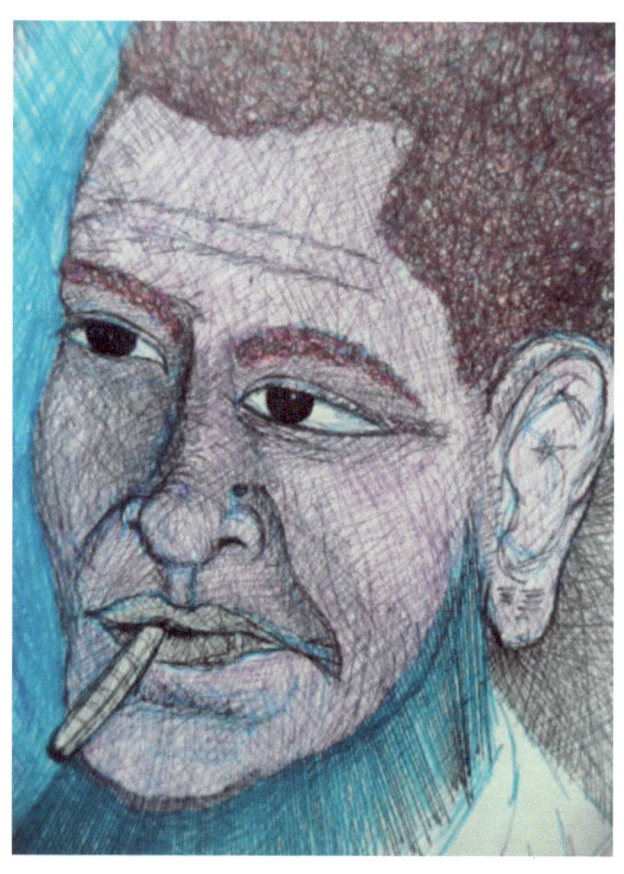

I smoked dope all through college …
but never while sleeping!!!

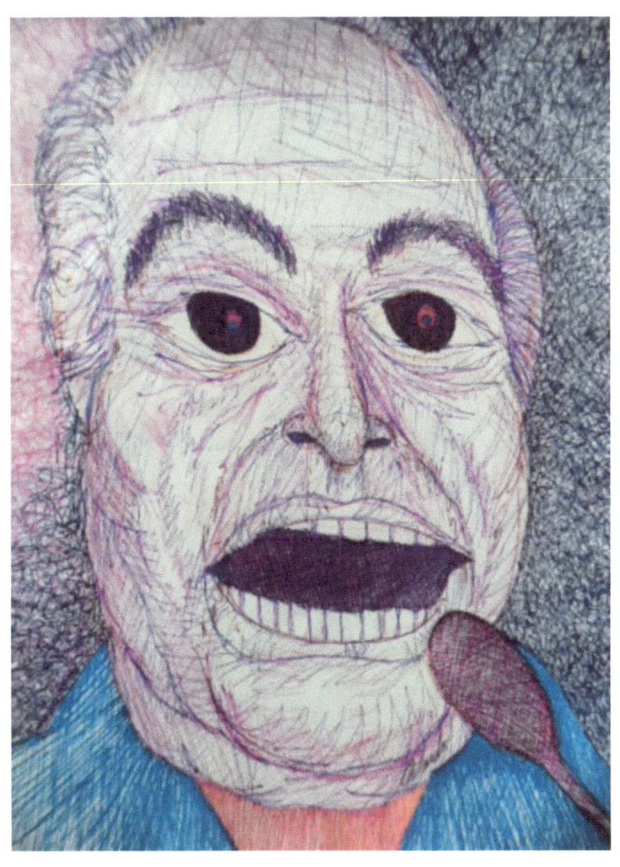

Don't blame me! ... I didn't vote for that IDIOT!!!!

The only thing you need to know is the
difference between SHIT and SHINOLA!!!!

If BARACK would only roll the price of gas back to $2.OO per gallon; THE ECONOMY WOULD FIX ITSELF!!!!

I WILL!!! ... TURN AMERICA INTO A
THIRD WORLD NATION!!!

It's not because he's BLACK! …
It's because he's STUPID!!!!

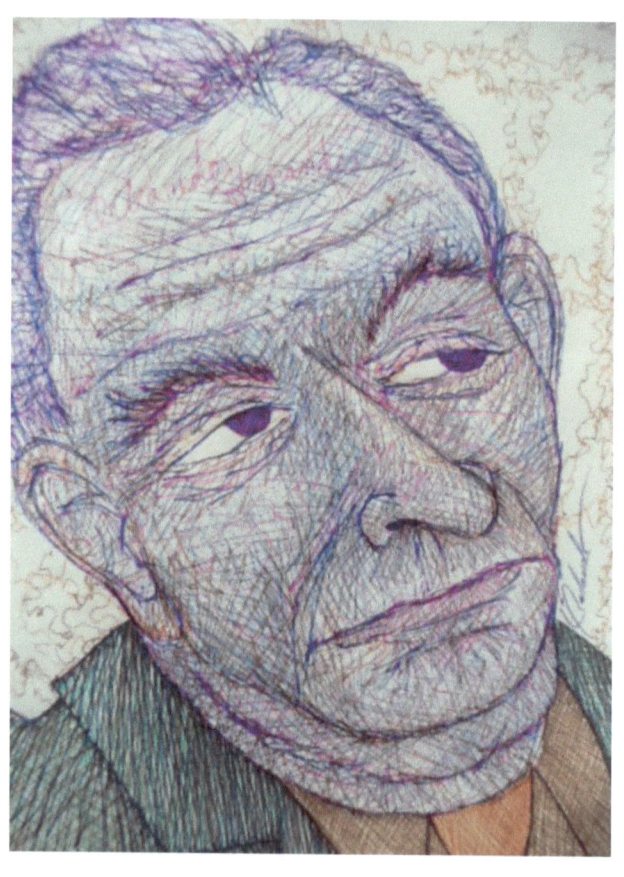

WE CAN'T EAT health care!!! …
What we need are JOBS!!!!

The Queen of England is lookin' SWEET!!!!! ….
Wonder if she wants to play??

OBAMA is a PIMP!! … Like SNOOP DOG!!!

I hope you enjoyed my *First Book* of political cartoons. If so, I would appreciate it if you would leave a review on the website where you purchased the book.

First Book – Vol. 2 now available.

Orlando Hernandez

www.ingramcontent.com/pod-product-compliance
Lightning Source LLC
Chambersburg PA
CBHW050839290526
45792CB00001B/455